S0-AHT-661

Laughter in the Walls

BOOKS BY BOB BENSON

Laughter In The Walls

Come Share The Being

Something's Going On Here

In Quest Of The Shared Life

He Speaks Softly

Disciplines For The Inner Life
(With Michael W. Benson)

"See you at the house."
(Edited by R. Benson)

Laughter in the Walls

BOB BENSON

Edited & Illustrated By Laura Leigh Benson-Greer

GENEROUX NELSON
Nashville

This book was originally published in 1969. For this revised edition, a small number of the original poems were replaced by a number of new poems written since the original collection was published. Some of those new poems first appeared in *Meanings,* a newsletter published from 1982-1986 by the author, and in *"See you at the house."*, a collection of the writer's best stories published in 1986 by Generoux, Inc.

The original watercolors are by Laura Leigh Benson-Greer.

Design & production of this book was ably executed by Schatz + Schatz (Nashville) based on a design by Ken Spradley of Design Communications (Nashville). The type is Administer and was set by QC Type, Inc. (Nashville). The film for the book was done by CSI (Nashville), the printing was done by Berryville Graphics, (Berryville, Va.). To each of the craftspeople involved, our gratitude.

LAUGHTER IN THE WALLS. Copyright © 1990 by Bob Benson. All rights reserved. Written permission must be secured to use or reproduce any part of this book, except for brief quotations in critical reviews or articles. For information, address Generoux, Inc., Post Office Box 158531, Nashville, Tennessee 37215.

Published in Nashville, Tennessee, by GENEROUX NELSON, an imprint of Thomas Nelson Publishers (Nashville), and distributed in Canada by Lawson Falle, Ltd., Cambridge, Ontario. Printed in the United States of America.

This is a first edition.

LIBRARY OF CONGRESS CATALOG-IN-PUBLICATION DATA
Benson, Bob.
  Laughter in the walls / Bob Benson; edited and illustrated by
  Laura Leigh Benson-Greer.
     p. cm.
   "Originally published in 1969."
   ISBN 0-8407-7449-4
   I. Benson-Greer, Laura Leigh. II. Title
  PS3552.E5476628L38 1990
  811'.54—dc20

90-6372
CIP

To those
who put it there.

Contents.

Foreword.

Normally, I am not the writer of the family.

However, I do have several important roles. Because of my many attempts to fix everything for everybody and to give further instruction to my ever-needy brothers, Dad pegged me early on as vice-mother. And I have done my best to live up to that title. Because of my tendency to trip at least twice a day, I am known as the family klutz. I have added a lot of creativity and class to that role through the years. Perhaps my best performance being the time I tripped on the sidewalk and fell headfirst into an electrician's tent, landing squarely in the electrician's lap.

I am also the painter of the family and so I was chosen to do the illustrations for this book. And because I am technically the editor as well, I was chosen to write the foreword for this revised edition of my father's first and most well-known book.

It was actually my brother Robert's idea that it would be neat to have some illustrations to go along with the poems and so he asked me to paint them. Anyone who knows me well knows that I am a chicken when it comes to showing my work to anyone, even members of my immediate family, so the idea of printing them in a book was scary to me. I decided to do it partly because it is difficult for anyone to pass up the chance to have their paintings in print.

Mostly though, I guess I wanted to do it because it gave me a way to work on a project with my dad and to say something about the life that we all had together when my brothers and I were growing up on Bayshore Drive.

I remember the past in terms of colors. Sunny golden days when we rolled down the hill in sleeping bags and carried picnics down to the patio at the lake. Windy gray days when we built tents in the hall upstairs and pretended to go camping. Soft green Saturdays in the spring when I would wake up and walk across the wet grass to where Dad was working in the garden so that I could get a good morning kiss. The crystal white day when Patrick first came home from the hospital by way of a tractor and a wheelbarrow over the snow.

So while there are better artists in the world, there are not other artists who remember what I think these poems are.

I have always loved these poems for the memories that they bring to mind. But they have come to mean more than that to me now for they carry with them the truths that Dad spent his life trying to share with us–simple truths about living and about loving. Dad's gift was in knowing that the most important truths in life are realized in the midst of the ordinary, everyday experiences that we all have.

So, as I struggle to write the papers and read the books that come with being a graduate student and to do the laundry and pick up the stuff that comes with being a mother and to pack the books and move around the paperwork that comes with helping to run a small publishing company, I can hear the words of my father reminding me that none of these things are the important things about my life. What matters is the talks and the laughter and the tears and the songs and the walks and the colors that I share with my husband and my son and the time I spend being quiet enough to hear the voice of God.

Dad once said (in this very book, in fact) that he knew he was just a bit player in life and that he had only been given a few short lines in the play. And that he only hoped that he would say those lines well.

I know now, Dad, that the way you lived and the words you said taught me things I had only begun to realize at the time. And I thank you, Dad, for the lines well said and the life well lived.

And I thank you for the colors.

Laura Leigh Benson-Greer
April, 1990

The Things I Believe.

I've lain in the grass
    on a soft spring morning
  with life chirping
    and buzzing around me.
And these were the things
    I said to the buttercups
  and the crocuses
    and sang to the robins.

I've walked into a
    dimly-lit room at night
  illuminated only by the rays
    of a Donald Duck night light.
And these were the things
    I whispered
  over the sleeping forms
    of my little boys.

I was out to the edge
    for a moment once,
  out where they say
    you have something
      we don't have a cure for.
And faced with the separation
    from loved ones,
  with uncompleted tasks
    and unfulfilled dreams,
  these were the things
    that brought me warmth
      and hope
        and comfort.

These are the things
    that I believe about God.

I'm more than just toenails
    and whiskers and elbows
    and a social security number.
Way down deep inside
    these things pull me together
    and make me a "me."
I am a measure of the truth
    that I have adopted.
And I have believed these things
    until there is no distance
      between me and them.
One by one
    I have stripped away
      doubts and questions
  until I have possessed these truths
and they have possessed me.

And if you could put your ear
    up tight against my heart
  when trials and darkness
    have stilled me to a whisper,
  or if you were there
    when joy burst forth
      in such a loud song
    that you had to back away,
  these are the things
    that you would hear
      from my voice
    and from my very being.

These are the things
    that are really me,
  they are the things I believe
    about God.

Obligation.

When I was a little boy,
    there was a time or two
I thought I had taken
    all an eight-year-old
      should have to take—
baths, yard-mowing,
    trash-hauling, orders,
Sunday School, piano lessons,
    and babysitting with sisters.
The only thing that kept me
    from running away
      was the fact
    that Mom wouldn't let me
      cross the street.
But I resolved to get a job,
    or rather a position,
    and pay them back for everything
      they had ever done for me—
      meals, bicycles,
    swimming suits,
      ballcaps, shoes,
    skates, rent—
      everything.
And then maybe
    they would let me
      run my own life.

But even then
    I sorta wondered
    how I'd put a price
      on bedside vigils,
      kisses and bandaids
for skinned knees and elbows,
    on puzzles, games,
      bedtime stories,
    ice cream cones,
love, concern, worry, tears,
    crackling fires in the winter,
      fans in the summer,
and all the other things
    so plainly above and beyond
      the call of parental duty.

Almost daily I still find
    some hidden attitude
      or habit or value
that comes to me
    because of a good name given.
And I am made to realize
    an ever-deepening obligation
    to share a heritage
      with those
      who call me Dad.

Life Is So Daily.

Nearly everything I do
    needs doing again so soon.

Most everything I did today
    has to be redone tomorrow
or at least
    by the end of the week.
Shaving, eating,
    driving to work,
    cleaning the gutters,
    building a fire,
    answering the mail,
    keeping up with the Joneses,
    talking on the phone.

All these,
    and a hundred other things,
make up my waking hours
day after day,
    week after week.
Until at times it seems that
    most of my life is spent
in a succession of marches
    that do not matter
and numberless causes
    that do not count.

And I am made to wonder:
    Will I give myself away
    bit by bit—
time, thought,
    energy, love,
    emotion, will—

to a collection
    of choices and projects
which will die as I do,
    because they mattered only
    to me?

Somehow may I use
    the lumber of my life
to build a ladder—
    straight, sturdy, true—
on which people may climb
    until they come to thee.
Or to fashion a cathedral—
    a quiet, holy place
where people would pause
    and seek thy ways.
Or to plant a tree—
    tall, serene, fruitful—
whose shade would someday
grant a traveler rest.

Let me share
    in thy works,
    not asking that I must see
    the results in my day,
but laboring
    in this confidence:
Because it was done in thee,
    it will someday
    come to fulfillment
and I will not have lived
    worthlessly, selfishly,
    needlessly.

He Said His Lines.

One of our sons, Mike,
    wanted to take private speech.

He's such a talker anyway,
    I recommended *hush* instead.
But it was inexpensive
    and he was interested,
    so we let him.

The climax of the year's labor
    was a two-hour assortment
  of clowns, kings, rabbits,
    and forgotten lines
  known as the Speech Recital,
    given to a devoted audience
      of eager parents
        and trapped friends.
Mike was a king.
    He looked rather regal, too,
    if I do say so myself.
At least until the queen,
    a head taller and
      twenty pounds heavier,
  stood beside him
    casting a pall on his regality.
He had only three lines to say—
    nine months of speech,
    three short lines.
And they came very late,
    in the last moment
      of the last act
        of the very last play.

Anyway you looked at it,
    he was not the star.
At least not to anyone except
    a couple about halfway back
    on the left side.

It was a long evening
    and it was miserably hot.
But Mike waited
    and he was ready
  and he said his lines
    and he said them well.
Not too soon, not too late,
    not too loud, not too soft,
  but just right,
    he said his lines.

I'm just a bit player, too,
    not a star in any way.
But God gave me a line or so
    in the pageant of life,
  and when the curtain falls
    and the drama ends,
  and the stage is vacant at last,
    I don't ask for a critic's raves
    or fame in any amount.
I only hope that he can say,
    "He said his lines.
Not too soon, not too late,
    not too loud, not too soft.
He said his lines
    and he said them well."

Trophies And Tarnish.

You've had a good year, Bob.

A starting position,
    a trip to the regionals,
    trophies, medals, honors,
        recognition from
            your friends and teachers.
It was an impressive list
        of accomplishments
        for a sixteen-year-old.
And they were won
        in open competition,
    at a price in toil, study,
        and sweat.
But trophies tarnish
        and honors fade.
Already a sophomore has his eye
        on jersey number thirty-four
    and some kid
            has made up his mind
            to push you further back
                in the class.

Sooner or later someone
        will score more baskets,
    and do better
        than you have done.
So the important thing really
        is not the deed well done
    or the medal that you possess,
        but the dedication and dreams
            out of which they grow.

You must have a left-handed layup,
        a behind-the-back pass,
    a high percentage
        from the line,
            and a fall-away jumper.
But you must always have words
        that stir the imagination,
    thoughts that haunt your mind,
        and dreams that fill your heart.

For out of dreams,
        deeds grow.

Multiple Me's.

Most of the time it seems
  there is just not enough of me
    to go around.

At the office it is almost as if
  I leave more to do
    than I am ever able
      to get done.
And when I'm home,
  the yard,
  the family,
    the woodpile,
  the garage
    all seem to have
  a rightful claim on my time.
All of the projects
  I would like to be able
    to begin,
    the books I'd like to read,
  could all be done
    if there were only
      more of me to do them.

But then there are times
  where there are
    just too many of me.
One of those times
  is when I pray.
If only Bob the sincere,
  the quiet,
    the desirer of holy things
  could make his way alone
    to the place of prayer
  and make his petitions known.

And there find
  the power and poise
    his heart must have.

But every time he goes to pray,
  a whole multitude of me
  comes trooping right along—
    Bob the impatient,
      Bob the referee heckler,
  Bob the unconcerned,
    and the ambitious Bob
    and the unkind Bob.
And by the time
  they all crowd into the closet,
there is such a din and clamor
  that I can hardly hear
    the voice of God.
And then I am made to see
  that what I am in my thoughts,
  at work,
    at play,
      in traffic,
all these people
  make up the person I am
  when I kneel down to pray.

Oh, that I would love him so dearly
  that every moment of my life,
    ease, thought, pain,
      pleasure, toil, dreams—
would be but a preparation
  for those times
    when I shall be alone
      with him.

Digging.

God and I raised a flower bed.

He really did the most I guess
    because we used his soil,
  his air, his water,
    his life, his sun.
My part seemed so trivial
    that I said,
  "Lord, you take those bulbs
    and make them grow
  right here in the box
    out in the garage.
You don't need me, Lord,
    you can do it by yourself."
"No," he said,
    "I want to do my part,
  I'm waiting to begin,
    but you must do yours too.
You'll have to
    dig the bed,
  bury the bulbs,
    pull the weeds."
"Okay," I said,
    and I did my feeble part.

And God took those bulbs,
    burst them with life,
  fed them with soil,
    showered them with rain,

drew them with sunshine,
    until we had beautiful flowers.
And then he seemed to say,
    "Your life is like a garden,
And if you'd like,
    we'll make it a beautiful thing.
I'll furnish the soil of grace,
    the sunshine of love,
  the rains of blessing,
    the wonder of life,
  but you must do the digging."

"Lord, you just go ahead,
    make me what
    you want me to be.
Make me a saint,
    fill me with compassion,
    give me great faith."
"No," he said,
    "You've got to
  keep your heart tilled,
    hoe the weeds of evil,
  chop away the second-best."

"I'll make you anything.
    Pure, clean,
  noble, useful,
    anything you want to be.
    But only if you dig."

19.

Practicing The Presence.

A great composer hears music
   and writes it down
  that others may hear it too.
A great artist sees beauty
   and puts it on a canvas
  that others may enjoy it also.
A devout Christian feels a Presence
   and lives their life
    like they're not alone
  that others may know him too.

People often pray:
   "We beseech thee to come."
When the real prayer should be:
   "Thou art here,
    help me to sense it."

The simple truth is,
   as a dimpled baby,
    a mischievous child,
    a perplexed teenager,
    a harried adult,
  you never leave
   the presence of God
    for he is always near.
The problem
   is to know it.
Like inspiration
   to the musician, the artist,

these times of awareness,
   spiritual perception,
  seem to come and go
   in one's life.
And at times I am swept away
   in the grace of communion,
    the posture of praise.
Times of almost inexpressible joy,
   overwhelming fellowship,
   uncontrollable song.
They come not as often as I'd like,
   not every time I wish it so.
But they come unannounced
   like the calling winds,
    the refreshing showers.
Then suddenly they're gone
   and I am "me" again.
"Me" with a family to feed,
   with a living to make.
But somehow "me"
   a little stronger,
    a little better,
   for having been with him.
But I cannot help but wonder
   what kind of person
    I could be
  if daily, hourly
   or "alway-ly,"
  I could learn to walk with him.

I Never Took A Step.

It was Pioneer Day.

Our town's answer to
   the Rose Parade,
     the All-Star Game,
   the World's Fair,
     and the Mardi Gras
  all rolled into one colorful
   but tiring day.
Between helping with the fish fry,
   Peg's aid in the cake sale,
  boys in the all-star games,
   Mike in different costumes
     for parade and pageant,
  it was a very busy day.

I was on the sidewalk,
   camera ready and focused
     for Mike
  who would come clowning
   down the street.
I waited through bands,
   army tanks, ponies,
     majorettes, and floats
  but no sign of Mike.
So I waited through motorcycles,
   drill teams, Indians, stray dogs,
  and a dozen other clowns,
   but still no Mike.
I finally found Mike
  at the parade's dispersal.

His face was a combination of
   freckles, grease paint,
     perspiration,
      and shame.
"I chickened out," he said.
   "How far did you ride?"
"I never took a step."

Suddenly, I remembered days
   I'd started out
     with high resolve
  to carry the Master's banner
   in the procession of life.
And nights that found me
   defeated, discouraged,
     ashamed,
   knowing that I'd never
     taken a step for him.
And remembering
   the flood of compassion,
     mercy, kindness and grace
   which he gave,
  I said to Mike,
   "There will be other days
     and other parades.
  You're still the finest clown
   I know."
Mike's face burst into smiles,
   my heart burst into song,
   and just for a moment I knew
   the joy of Christlikeness.

Hearts And Treasures.

Spring is here.

The young are smitten with love,
   the ground is
     covered with greenery,
  and the garage is
   bursting with junk.
Where did it all come from
   and where is it all going?

With the advent
   of cleaning time,
  attics everywhere
   are "crowdedly testifying"
  that as human beings
   we are accumulators,
    collectors, junk dealers.
And our assortment of goods—
   whether it be hats, houses,
  clothes, cameras,
   furniture, lamps—
the Master called our treasure.

He didn't call it treasure
   because of its usefulness.
Lovely chairs minus one leg,
   lots of jars without any tops,
  magazines old enough
   to be in a barber shop.

And not because of its value
   did he call it treasure.
They'd charge you to haul it off.

But treasure, he said,
   because they are pictures
  of places where you put
   your heart for a while.
They were all things
   you could not do without,
    that you just had to have.
Remember the day
   you signed the notes?
The painful monthly payments
   to buy this collection of things
   you no longer use?
They were treasures then,
   but just like he said,
  moths and time,
   rust and kids,
    thieves and the dog
  have reduced them
   to spring cleaning projects.
Basements, attics, carports,
   eloquently echoing
  the timeless words of the Master:
  "Be careful what you treasure.
For where your treasure is
   your heart will be."

The Big News.

The newspaper headlines
    screamed the news.
Big, bold, black, front page—
    SHEPARD SUCCESSFUL
      IN VAULT INTO SPACE.
But the real news,
    the big, big story,
  was tucked away neatly
    on the bottom corner
     of page seven.
BENSON:
    Mr. & Mrs. Robert G.,
111 Haven Street, Hendersonville,
  Lori Leigh, born May 2nd,
    Baptist Hospital.

There's nothing so important
    about her, you say.
  Well, she thinks there is.
She has completely
    rescheduled the family,
  taken over the den,
    claimed a refrigerator shelf.

I think she's important too.
  Important because she's mine.
Mine to love—
    tiny fingers,
     dimpled chin,
    shining eyes.
Mine to care for—
    food and thoughts,

   clothes and faith,
     school and habits.
She's plenty important to me.

She's important to God, too,
    important because she's his.
Yes, Lori Leigh
    and Kathi Ann,
     James Alan,
    Terri Leah,
  and all of the seventeen new folk
    on the cradle roll.
For people
    are more important to God
     than accomplishments.
What does he care
    about moonshots,
  world championships,
    space rides?
These are just
    deeds to be outdone,
  records to be broken,
    events to be overshadowed.
But these little folk
    will dwell with him forever.

The big story is not always
    on the front page.
  The real news,
    the big stories,
are about people.
    People like Lori Leigh.

Tardiness.

You were late
    but I wasn't alarmed
    because you are always late.
I can't exactly remember
    if you made the wedding
        on time
    but if per chance
        you did come down
            the aisle promptly,
    it was one of the last times.

You said you'd meet me
        at seven
    and we'd have dinner,
        just the two of us.
So I laid out enough work
    to last until seven-thirty.
Seven came
        but you didn't.
The clock said seven forty-five
        but the empty street below
            said you hadn't arrived
    and I found myself
        leaning back in my chair
    with the work pushed aside,
        looking up the street
            for the station wagon
                and you.

Surprising how much
    of one's life
        can go by
            in a few minutes.
Flashbacks of meetings
    we had had after work,
        for lunch,
        home from traveling,
            after an hour,
        after a day,
            after a week.
But every time
    with the same little quickness
        in my throat
    that I felt as I waited
        for you now for dinner.

You came
    and we ate,
laughed and talked
    and went home.
And you,
    who probably knows me
        better than anyone else
            in the world,
    didn't even suspect
        what it meant to me
    to see you
        coming down the street
            at seven forty-seven.

Instant Obedience.

There are three ways
    to get to our dining room—
up from the living room,
    through the hall,
        or in from the kitchen.
The conventional route
    to the breakfast table
is down the stairs,
    through the hall,
        and there you are.
It's the easiest, it's closest,
    you just keep bearing right
        and lean your way in.
The other morning
    when Peg called,
I was first to come down to eat.
    Bobby, Mike, & Leigh followed.
On impulse I stood up
    on Leigh's highchair
        in the corner,
    ready to surprise them
        as they came through the hall.
I heard them
    thunder down the steps,
my muscles tensed
    for the pounce.
For reasons unknown to me,
    they made a hard left turn
        and I had been flanked.
But I was up there so I just stayed
    trying to look as if
I were waiting for a trolley
    or something sensible.
Bobby and Mike,
    eleven and eight,
sophisticated men of the world,
    ignored me completely.

But two-year-old Leigh
    smiled and said,
    "Hi, Dad. Whatcha doing?"
Now it's not too easy
    to explain why at 7:20 a.m.,
you, a responsible adult,
    are standing, of all places,
        in a highchair.
"Leigh, I'm waiting up here
    to jump on you.
    Lie down. Here I come,
        right in the middle
            of your tummy."
Quick as a flash
    she was down on the floor.
In another instant
    I sat beside her,
rejoicing in this tribute
    of confidence, devotion,
        and trust
in one of her dad's plans
    for the moment.

O Lord, help me
    to love you so much
    to trust you so completely,
        that if you said,
    "Lie down, boy,
    I'm going to
        run over you,"
    I too would obey
        instantly—completely.
May the quality
    of my devotion
    and the depth
        of my confidence
    make thy great heart glad.

Paternal Instinct.

"Tom," I said
　　as I looked down at him,
　"You can't say a word,
　　or play a game,
　　　or put on your shirt,
　　　　or fix your supper.
You don't have a car or a job
　　or go to school—
　and besides,
　　you're expensive.
The price of babies
　　seems to be steadily rising
　　　since '52—Bobby,
　　　'56—Michael,
　　　　'61—Leigh.
You'd think I'd
　　get some discount.
"And, Tom,
　　you're time-consuming.
You won't eat
　　what the rest of us do
　　　or when, either.
There you are,
　　my new son,
　just a helpless, broke,
　　expensive, noisy
　　　bundle of humanity.
But you can be
　　a happy baby,
　　　an active boy,
　an exuberant teenager,
　a useful man,
　if someone will take the time

to feed you, clothe you,
　guide you, teach you,
　　paddle you, love you,
　　　train you.
For you are also one of life's
　　choice opportunities,
　a rich and challenging way
　　in which to serve God.
If I fail you,
　　there is no way
　for me to be
　　a real success.
But if I train you well—
　　in wisdom,
　　　in faith,
　　in courage,
　　　in honesty—
I will have risen above
　　all other failures."

With these great odds at stake,
　　my heart is made to pray:

O thou, who through
　　thy miracle of life
　hast bestowed
　　this honor on me,
　grant me
　　one more request:
Give me thy grace,
　　thy understanding,
　　　thy love.
Make me a father like thee.

Prejudice.

Everybody says
    our newest son,
  Patrick Copeland Benson,
    is a strikingly beautiful baby.
I readily agree
    but then I do have a question
      about my judgment
because I thought all of our children
    were beautiful babies.
I felt that Bobby, our first-born,
    was the handsomest thing
      I had ever seen anywhere.
But fourteen years later,
    as I look at snapshots
      of his tiny face,
  I either had a very cheap camera
    or he was just barely average.
But at the time,
    as a proud new father,
  I saw him with eyes
    so completely prejudiced
      and blinded by love,
    it was pure delight
      to look at him.

And it brings no end
    of consolation and strength
      to my heart
to remember that when
    the heavenly Father
      looks at me,
he doesn't see
    the modest victories,
resounding defeats,
    courageous aspirations,
faltering results,
    noble motives,
      shabby attitudes,
    optimistic starts,
and discouraging stops
    that are so much
      a part of me.

But he looks
    through eyes of love.
And in his sight
    I am transformed
    to a useful, worthy,
      noble being.

Shadow.

From the time little boys are born
    until they are three or so,
   they belong to their moms.
But the next three years
    belong to their dad.
I have one of those
    three plus-ers at my house.
If I wear a shirt,
    he wears a shirt.
If I go barefooted,
    he goes barefooted.
If I read, he reads.
    If I dig, he digs.
He doesn't ask to go fishing
    or to the park or swimming,
   it seems enough for him
    just to be with me.
I look forward to the weekends
    with delight
   because he will not be more
    than three steps behind me.

When life beats me down a bit
    and I lose the confidence
     to lead,
    to master,
     to choose,
I sometimes come home
    and just walk around the yard
with Tom
    a step or two behind.
Somehow just to feel
    his trust,
     his confidence,
    his devotion,
   gives me strength
    to try some more.

You can't fool a little boy
    about character
   and I just accept his judgment
    that there must be
     something to me after all.

Laughter In The Walls.

I pass a lot of houses
  on my way home.
Some pretty,
  some expensive,
   some inviting.

But my heart always skips a beat
  when I turn down the road
and see my house
  nestled against the hill.

I guess I'm especially proud
  of the house
   and the way it looks
  because I drew the plans myself.
It started out large enough for us—
  I even had a study,
two teenage boys
  now reside in there.
And it had a guest room,
  my girl and nine dolls
   are permanent guests.
It had a small room
  Peg had hoped
would be her sewing room,
  the two boys swinging
   on the dutch door
have claimed this room
  as their own.

So it really doesn't look right now
  as if I'm much of an architect.
But it will get larger again.

One by one they will go away—
  to work, to college,
   to service,
    to their own houses.
And then there will be room—
  a guest room, a study,
   and a sewing room—
for just the two of us.

But it won't be empty.
  Every corner, every room,
  every nick in the coffee table
  will be crowded
   with memories.
Memories of picnics,
  parties, Christmases,
   bedside vigils, summers,
  fires, winters, going barefoot,
   leaving for vacation, cats,
    conversations, black eyes,
graduations, first dates,
  ballgames, arguments,
   washing dishes, bicycles,
  dogs, boat rides,
getting home from vacation,
  meals, rabbits,
and a thousand other things
  that fill the lives
of those who would raise five.
And Peg and I
  will sit quietly by the fire
and listen to the
  laughter in the walls.

31.

Second Helpings.

His prayers
    are not always the same.
Some nights he prays,
    "Now I lay me
        down to sleep..."
Simple words,
    but words of dignity
        from his young heart.
Other nights he begins,
    "Our Father
        which art in heaven..."
And he perfectly repeats those
    beautiful life-giving words.
But the nights I like best
    are the nights
        he extemporizes
    and this was one
        of those choice nights.
As a parent your heart leaps
    from laughter to tears
        and back again.
"Lord," he prayed,
    "Give us this day..."
Stymied momentarily, he paused.
    Then in a flash of insight
        he resumed,
    "Lord, give us
        some other days too."
Later on
    I found myself echoing
    this bit of seven-year-old wisdom,
        "Give me some tomorrows
            too, Lord."
But at our house
    we have a rule
    which now marched erect
        past me.

No extras,
    no "mores,"
        no "seconds,"
    until the "firsts" are gone.
No more bacon
    until you've downed the egg.
No more steak
    until you eat the spinach.
And now this rule
    that I had made for them
        thrust itself on me.
Do I deserve another day,
    another set of blessings?
    Is today's plate clean?
Twenty-four hours,
    fourteen hundred and
        forty minutes,
    eighty-six thousand and
        four hundred seconds—
    all mine.
To use, to abuse,
    to account for.

Oh, Lord,
    help me to take today.
May I, with dedication,
    use its opportunities,
        accept the reverses,
    share its burdens.
May I be
    thankful for its graces,
    humble in its successes,
        devoted to its Giver.
May I, in some measure,
    earn tomorrow
    by the way I live
        today.

Openhandedness.

There is something about fall—
   the turning trees,
    the crisp nights,
   the clear mornings,
    the football games,
   the chrysanthemums—
that makes me feel
   I like her best
   of all the seasons.
At least I always think so
   after a long, hot summer.

And yet with all her beauty—
   trees, flowers
  and her sweet relief
   from heat and grass cutting—
  she arouses in my heart
   a faint sadness, a poignancy.
As the year
   heads down the stretch
  and the days grow shorter,
   she seems to quietly say,
  "There's a time to plant,
   a time to grow,
    a time for winter's blast."

I learned this feeling early,
   this sense of "mortalness."
When I was a boy,
   there was no joy
  quite like that which
   a sunny Saturday morning
   brought.

There was fishing and games
   and swimming
  and cowboys and Indians
   and mud between your toes.
But the hours raced by
   and in my childish heart
  I knew there was
   a time to play,
    to swim, to run, to laugh,
  but the darkness was coming
   and the bathtub waited,
  and I felt an inner pain
   because I could not halt
   the day.

And I know it now.
   I look at them—
Bob, Mike, Leigh, Tom, Pat—
   seated around my table
  and my heart wells up
   with pride, joy, happiness
  marred only by this faint pang,
   that the moments
    I clutch to myself
  are so swiftly passing by.
Oh, to be able
   to release these moments
   into his hand.
Gladly, unbegrudgingly, freely,
   like a tree sheds its leaves.
Happy, secure, in this certainty—
   that in his plan
  there's always another spring.

Parental Math.

Nearly a week ago, Peg and I
    had a very hard week.

    Wednesday night—
Mike slept downstairs
    in his room
    where children belong
    and we slept upstairs in ours
    where moms and dads belong.
    Thursday night—
We were 350 miles away
    and he was in Ramada 325
    and we were in 323
    in connecting rooms
    and we left the door open
    and talked and laughed
        together.
    Friday night—
700 miles from home
    and he was in 247
    and we were in 239 but it was
    just down the balcony
    and somehow
    we seemed together.

    Saturday night—
He was in the freshman dorm
    and we were still in 239.
    Sunday night—
We were home
    and he was 700 miles away
        in Chapman 309.

Now we have
    been through this before.
Robert had gone away to college
    and we had gathered
        ourselves together
    until we had gotten over it.
Mainly because
    he is married now
    and he only lives ten miles away
        and comes to visit often.

So we thought we knew
    how to handle separation
        pretty well
    but we came away so lonely
        and blue.

Oh, our hearts
  are filled with pride
    at a fine young man
  and our minds
    are filled with memories
  from tricycles
    to commencements
  but deep down inside somewhere
    we just ached
      with loneliness and pain.

Somebody said
  you still have three at home.
Three fine kids and
    there is still plenty of noise,
  plenty of ballgames to go to,
    plenty of responsibilities,
      plenty of laughter.
Plenty of everything,
  except Mike.

And in parental math,
  five minus one
    just doesn't equal plenty.

And I was thinking about God.
    He sure has plenty
      of children.
Plenty of artists,
    plenty of singers
      and carpenters
  and candlestick makers
    and preachers.
Plenty of everybody,
    except you.
And all of them together
    can never take your place.
And there will always be
    an empty spot in his heart
  and a vacant chair at his table
    when you're not home.

And if once in a while
    it seems as if
  he's crowding you a bit,
    try to forgive him.
It may be one of those nights
    when he misses you so much
      he can hardly stand it.

35.

Skipping Rocks.

It was a bright,
    sunshiny morning,
   the first of ten days off for me.
And I was out in the yard early,
    working on a wall
     down by the lake.
Knee deep
    in pleasant, warm water,
   I could hardly have been happier
    or more at peace.

Patrick came down
    and began to throw rocks
     in the water.
You don't have to teach
    little boys to throw rocks,
   they just seem to be born
    with both the skill
     and the desire.
He wanted me
    to stop and play with him,
"Teach me how
    to make them skip."
"In a little while," I said.
    "Let me get a little more
     of this wall built."
After a while,
    he got tired of waiting
   and started up the hill
    to the house.
I figured he'd be back
    in a few minutes.

But later in the morning
    when I went up for a drink,
   he was in bed
    with a high fever.
It turned out to be
    a very serious illness
   that was to spread
    through the whole family,
not to mention my vacation.
It took some of us to the hospital
    and all of us to bed.
Fortunately for us,
    it was all over
     in a month or so,
   having run its course
    with no lingering effects.
And there have been other days
    and other chances
   to skip rocks with Patrick.

But I can still see him
    trudging up that hill,
   a long pull for his short legs,
    and I'm reminded
that you never know
    they're coming back.
There aren't any guarantees.
    And the only time
you really know
    you can skip rocks
is when you're saying
    "in a little while."

Disparity.

I started to pull them up
    and throw them away—
  the brown, lifeless remains
    of twelve shrubs.

I had planted them
    with pride and expectation.
Now they were slain
    by our severest winter
    of the century.
But like most things I do,
    I put it off.
And March brought
    some bright sunshine,
  the spring rain,
    a few warm nights.
And somehow,
    unbeknownst to me,
      life—
wondrous, mysterious, thrilling—
burst out of those brown stems
    until they, like all the world—
the trees, grass, buttercups—
    seemed to be saying,
  in spring's glorious message,
    "I love to live!"

People, too, have this
    ingrained love for life,
  a desire to remain,
    a dread of dying.
History is filled with stories
of men and women
    with nothing left to live for.
Possessions, health, friends,
    family, future, all gone.
But they clung to life dearly,
    grimly they tied
  one more knot
    in the end of the rope.
It runs deep, this desire
    for self-preservation,
  this dread of being snuffed out.

Then how do you explain
    a young man just thirty-three,
  in the prime of life,
    setting his face
    toward Jerusalem to die.
The birds were happily warbling
    their songs of spring,
  but he walked
  serenely,
    resolutely,
    triumphantly,
to a cross and death—
    cruel, agonizing,
    undeserved death.

"Herein is love...
    not that we loved him...
But that he loved us...
    the recompense
    for our sins."

Dedication.

Most of my writing
    is dedicated to Peg,
      of course.

An old-fashioned girl
    who said old-fashioned words
      with me,
  to love and to cherish.
And who has done so with style—
    for better, for worse,
      for richer and for poorer
        in sickness and in health—
  for three decades
    of our quest.
After all these years,
    five dear children,
  five grandchildren,
    fourteen jobs,
      five pastorates,
    fifteen moves later...
  it caught us by surprise.

We took each other's hands
    and clenched them together
  until our knuckles were white,
    knowing full well
  that we might not be able
    to hold on
      in spite of our resolve.

So we relaxed our grip
    and gently held hands
  in a loving, releasing way
    and suddenly
  we became more tightly bound
    than ever before.

By letting go,
    we held on.
By standing back,
    we drew closer.
By ceasing to clutch tomorrow,
    there is nothing like today.

Peeking At A Miracle.

Lacey, you made us stay up all night.

And for a grandfather
　　that is not as easy
　　　as it used to be.
Finally, at 4:10 a.m. or so,
　　Jacquelynn Lacey Benson,
　to address you properly
　　by your full name,
　your mom headed for the room
　　where you would be
　　　"delivered."

So there we all were,
　　a bedraggled bunch,
　filled with cups and cups
　　of vending machine coffee
　　　and hours and hours
　of CNN headline news.
An assortment of
　　maternal and paternal
　grandmothers, grandfathers,
　　aunts, uncles, and friends
　trying to look through
　　two tiny windows
　in the big doors that stood guard
　　over the long corridor.

We watched your mom
　　roll out of her room,
　she disappeared around a corner
　　past the nurses' station.

We saw them dress your dad up
　　like a spaceman—
　　　white crinkly overalls,
　　　　green hat and mask,
　　　big, blue booties.
Then the hall was empty
　　and quiet.

Now the intensity
　　of the waiting picked up.
I am sure the intensity
　　of the "delivering"
　　　was picking up too.
"I want to see the baby."
　　"I think it will be a girl."
　　"I can't wait."
An eternity of almost
　　twenty minutes went by
　and then around the corner
　　you came,
　nestled in the right arm
　　of your father,
　whose mask had been removed
　　to reveal an enormous smile
　　　of pride, awe and relief.
"It's a girl! Everybody is fine."

We crowded around for
　　our first glimpse of you,
　love at first sight
　　I must confess.
Your mom's nose,

your dad's dimple
on the miniature face
instantly devastated us all
before the nurse
gently led the entourage
on to the nursery door.
Tom and the nurse went inside.
The rest of us
hurried around to a window
where they promised
you would soon reappear.

I was standing with your daddy.
I guess I ought to warn you
about him.
He is as quick as a flash,
never without a retort
filled with humor.
He will have you laughing
a hundred thousand times
before he finally has to say,
in answer to some
preacher's question,
"Her mother and I."
But for this moment,
his mirth was gone,
swallowed up
by the deep sanctity
of the miracle
that had recently transpired
before his very eyes.
"I have never seen anything

quite like that before,"
were his quiet, reverent words.

I thought how right he was,
remembering mornings
in this very hospital
when the birthings of children
of my own,
including Tom,
had reconfirmed
the miracle of life.

For better or worse,
your dad has lived
in the era of television,
when the world has become,
as one described it,
a "19-inch neighborhood."
He has seen everything else—
murders, beatings,
men on the moon,
rapes, robberies,
men dying in battle,
fires in California,
starvation in India,
and riots and wrecks
and hostage taking.

Thank you, Lacey,
for reminding your dad,
as well as the rest of us,
life is the real miracle.

A Sweet Gum Tree.

It was a lovely summer morning.

The sky was blue,
    the sun shining,
      the breezes blowing.
It had been a hard week,
    replete with details,
     frustration,
    and late evening work.
And this day
    I couldn't get moving.
I was tired, nervous,
    just plain beat.
I made several starts at work
    but kept ending up
      on the front porch,
    piled on the lounge.
Lying there,
    I looked at the wind blow
      through the treetops.

Close by the front porch
    stands a sweet gum tree.
It looks as if at one time
    something nearly killed it
until now it is
    a strange combination
    of the lovely and the grotesque.
A part of the tree is alive,

    drinking in the rain,
    reaching for the sunshine,
      playing in the breezes.
And part of it is dead,
    unmoved, unfeeling,
      untouched
by the wonderful graces
    of God.

A sweet gum tree quietly
    showing me the way I was,
in stark contrast
    to the way that God
through his Spirit
    meant me to be.
A sweet gum tree causing me
    to breathe this prayer:

So fill me with thy life
    that I shall
  feel thy slightest touch,
    hear thy softest whisper,
 see thy faintest footprint,
    yielding in
      such glad response
that others might see
    the grace and beauty
of communion
    with thee.

All Them New Things.

Let me brag a little.

I have a grandson named
    Robert Green Benson III.
Now in case you're not big
    on family trees,
  that makes me
    Robert Green Benson, Sr.
And I have a son,
    Robert Green Benson, Jr.,
  and a grandson named
    Robert Green Benson III.

Before he was born
    we were duly notified
  that in the event
    the baby was a boy
      he would be so named
  and we were to call him
    Robert.
Peering across the gap
    between the generations
  I took this to mean
    we were not to make
      the same mistake

of re-using such terms
  as Bobby or Little Bobby
    or Baby Bobby,
      it was to be *Robert.*
It seemed like quite a handle to me
    for less than ten pounds
    of humanity.
It seemed very awkward to say,
    "Goochy-goochy, *Robert.*"

But Robert it was.
    Until somebody
  started calling him "Pookie"
  or just "Pook" for short.
Now Bobby sounds better to me
    than Pookie
    but then
    what do grandfathers know?

A little while
    after Robert was born,
  Tom, my ten-year-old,
    said to his mom,
      "Robert sure is lucky."
And Peg wanted to know

why Robert was so lucky
in Tom's mind.
"Because he gets to do
all them new things."
And now she wanted to know
what all those new things were
that Tom was referring to.
"Well," Tom began,
"he's never climbed a tree
or waded in the lake
or run through a field
or felt the wind in his face
or ridden a bicycle—
all them new things."

And later I was thinking
about all of God's children
and about our life in the Spirit.
About all the wonderful surprises
and stupendous things
he has for all of us to do
and see and feel and be
and how we just sit down
where we came in.
And about how we have

all the questions
and all the answers
and know all the things
to say and sing.
And about how we know
all the steps and plans
for everybody else
and their children too.
And about how we
rigidize and dilute.
And I wonder
how many new joys
and insights
and ways of punching holes
in the darkness
and poems and songs
and smiles
and simple pleasures
we miss.

Because we cannot
begin to conceive
how lucky we are.
Because in him there are
"all them new things."

Synopsis.

To look at me,
  138 pounds of pure dynamite,
you'd never know
  I used to be sickly.
But it's true,
  I had them all—
scarlet fever, flu,
  mumps, measles, hives,
    pneumonia, asthma
and a hundred others.
It seemed to me
  I was the first to catch it
    and the last to let it go.
During those days of quiet,
  I learned to love to read.
As a boy
  I sailed the high seas,
  braved raging storms,
    hacked through jungles,
and explored dark caves
  in hot pursuit of
    the Hardy Boys,
      Tow Sawyer,
    Nancy Drew,
  and other assorted heroes.
They always caught the villain,
  rescued the baby,
    won the battle,
  found the money,
    and lived happily
      ever afterwards.
As I grew older
  I began to read books
in which the hero died
  or the wrong guy married
    the fair young princess.
You know the kind,

  books with true-life endings.
I guess I'm sentimental,
  even childish,
    but I like books that end well.
Let the hero
  be down and nearly out,
  shot and left for dead,
    but let him win in the end.

And so I like the Bible
  because it ends well.
It begins with the heroes
  in a sinless, deathless land.
But they tripped, fell and
  began a downward journey
    that led through misery,
      failure, sorrow,
        and shame,
  until finally you say
    they'll never make it back.
But when it ends,
  they're home again.
It took God's Son to do it,
  but it ends well.
In these days,
  with the world divided
    into two camps
  glaring back and forth
    like two little boys
      across a line in the dust,
  with hatred, strife,
    wars and rumors,
  it's nice to know
    that the One who
      started it well
will also see that it ends
  according to his plan.

Days And Decades.

Where did they go,
    the days and the decades?

Days so filled with goodness
    we lived them like
        they always would be.
Days that brought
    such tiredness and hurt
we thought
    they would not pass.
Days when we scarcely knew
    whether to laugh or cry
because they marked
    beginnings and endings.
And decades that sped by
    so quickly
you had hardly learned to say 60
    when it was suddenly
        70 instead.
Decades marked
    in feet and inches in the hall.
Decades that brought
    peace and wisdom
        and shortness of breath.

Where did they go,
    the days and the decades?
Yesterday they were dependent
    on us for everything—
for counsel and protection.
Not long ago he wanted a bicycle,
    now he has
        a nine-year-old of his own.
Yesterday this one
    was squirming in church,
    last night he led the family
        in Christmas worship
        and communion.

Last night I put her to bed,
    tucked her in
        with her dolls and bears,
    now she's studying
        to be a doctor.
And the blonde,
    when I was in the yard
        on Saturdays,
    he stayed beside me,
now he has packed his truck
    and gone.
And the one
    we keep calling the "baby"
        is nearly seventeen.

Where did they go,
    the days and the decades?
They went to see Saint Nick
    and the tooth fairy
    and to ballgames and weddings
    and seminary and to work,
to Chicago and home again,
    on vacation to state parks
        and Europe,
    to college and Colorado
        and camp.
To parties and malls and hospitals
    and hundreds of other places
    where they are beyond retrieval
    even if I went again to look.
But a place to which
    they have also gone
is among the treasures
    of my heart,
filling my memory
    with richness and joy.
Gone indeed, but forever mine,
    the days and the decades.

About Bob Benson.

Bob Benson was born in Nashville, Tennessee in 1930, the son of a religious music publisher, the grandson of a charter member of the Church of the Nazarene. He was educated, for the most part, at Nazarene schools, including the Nazarene Theological Seminary in Kansas City. He was an ordained minister in the church and held pastorates in Florida, Missouri, California, and Tennessee.

In the early sixties, he returned to Nashville and joined his father in the family publishing business. Over the next twenty years, he became one of the Christian world's leading publishing executives. His efforts at the John T. Benson Publishing Company were characterized by a deep sensitivity for the quality of the published product and a pronounced emphasis on the quality of the ministry of the product itself.

Along the way, he came to be highly sought after as a speaker for retreats, conferences, and college campuses because of his warmth, his dry wit, and his keen insight. His unique ability to see the deep spiritual truths in the everyday occurrences of life earned him a place in the hearts of the thousands of people who heard him speak all over the country. As his reputation as a speaker grew, he began to write, publishing six books and a monthly newsletter over the course of his career.

In the late seventies, a sense of calling to spend his days speaking and writing on a full-time basis led him to resign from the publishing company. For a little more than six years, he traveled and wrote.

For many of the country's Christian artists and writers, as well as for pastors and lay leaders everywhere, Bob Benson was a friend, counselor, sounding board, chaplain, fellow pilgrim, and comrade-in-arms in the struggle to punch as many holes in the darkness as they could. He laughed with, created with, argued with, prayed with, corresponded with, and

retreated with enough of them to earn a place that few others will ever achieve.

In March, 1986, he finally lost one last battle to cancer, which he had fought valiantly for more than a dozen years. He, of course, would say that he won the war.

About Laura Leigh Benson-Greer.

Laura Leigh Benson-Greer is the only daughter, and therefore by her brothers' reckoning, was quite likely the favorite child of Bob Benson and easily the favorite sibling of the brothers themselves.

She paints watercolors professionally on commission, studies pastoral care at Vanderbilt Divinity School, writes term papers and sermons and other things worth reading, manages significant portions of the work of Generoux, and makes plans for a home that she and her musician husband and their son will someday build at the family farm north of Nashville.

She also collects hats with a passion, drives a pickup with style and grace, holds the title of most revered aunt to Peggy's grandchildren by acclamation, and continues her role of vice-mother to the aforementioned, and very grateful, brothers with a good deal of style and cheer.

About Generoux, Inc.

Generoux is a small Christian press formed to create platforms for uniquely gifted writers and speakers who might otherwise go unpublished and unheard. The company takes its name from the French word that means *openhandedness*—a favorite theme of its founding spirit, Bob Benson. For more information about Generoux, its writers, publications, and retreats, or to be placed on their mailing list, please contact Generoux, Inc., Post Office Box 158531, Nashville, Tennessee 37215 or telephone 615.889.8306.